T0153304

In Primary Light

In Primary
Light

p o e m s   b y

John Wood

UNIVERSITY OF IOWA PRESS Ψ IOWA CITY

University of

Iowa Press,

Iowa City 52242

Copyright © 1994

by John Wood

All rights reserved

Printed in the

United States of America

Design by Richard Hendel

No part of this book may be reproduced or used in any
form or by any means, electronic or mechanical, including
photocopying and recording, without permission in writing
from the publisher.

Printed on acid-free paper

Library of Congress Cataloging-in-Publication Data

Wood, John, 1947–

    In primary light: poems / by John Wood.

      p.   cm.

    ISBN 0-87745-450-7 (paper)

    I. Title.

PS3573.O594615   1994   93-46325

813'.54—dc20   CIP

98 97 96 95 94 P 5 4 3 2 1

for CAROL *and* DAFYDD

Contents

Acknowledgments

Grateful acknowledgment is made to
Harvey S. Shipley Miller and J. Randall Plummer
for permission to use a photograph from The
Miller-Plummer Collection of Photography for
the cover of this book and to the editors of the
following magazines in which some of these poems
first appeared: *Antaeus*, *Body Politic*, the *Kansas
Quarterly*, the *Pacific Review*, *Poetry*, *Poetry Now*,
the *Southern Review*, and *Swallow's Tale*.

In Primary Light

The Bitter Part of Heaven

They're all there: the man killed
by the pinball machine; the girl
who laughed to death; the dieting boy
who choked on a tapeworm wiggling up
in search of cakes and steak; and, of course, the babies—
the ones the ants, the mad chefs,
the anacondas, piranhas, and the threshing machines got.
This is heaven's bitter part
where all the dead from the *Enquirer*'s pages
are housed whole again but in anger
at irony and excess. Their eyeballs
have turned right again, hacked heads
have found their proper bodies, the mountains
of dog food ground by angry sons
or husbands have reconstituted.
But they brood and play out of tune,
pluck the wrong strings and frown
at those no tabloid ever eulogized.
It is hard for them being here
even though it's heaven,
things having gone quite wrong once,
irony having intruded
into an ordinary afternoon
like a steering wheel through the chest.
Some even say they would have done things

differently, things like sex, things
like that had they known it would have come to this:
a joke's butt reassembled with wings;
gowns of gossamer and gold stitching but a body
smooth as a mannequin's; a feeling of having been
betrayed. In other neighborhoods, others
who lived in fear of surprise,
waited on infected toenails and meteors,
the doors of saunas and freezers,
and then died boringly, old,
and on time, unable even to be surprised
that there was no surprise, fumble
through their songs like beginners,
though some have been at it for centuries.
They are distracted and equally bitter,
would have done things differently, too.
Of course, there are some areas
where hymns herald out of every window,
but there are few houses there
on those spare streets.

The Perils of Beauty

Pretty girl like lapdog—sometime go mad.
—from Charlie Chan in Rio

———————

No doubt a fair face, a fine
high bosom, or some glorious
buttocks' miraculous curve
has crazed down to bedlam
many a beauty, foamed up her lips,
snarled her smile, and snapped her mind
as easily as a string bean breaks
in the fingers of the kind of woman
whose mind is always safe, who now sits
on her porch, rocking beside
a heaped bushel, snapping
her supper and tomorrow's canning.

That beauty's peril lies beyond
any skeptic's doubt, beyond
the conundrums of cool, inscrutable sages,
is historical, incontestable, in Shakespeare,
and in her memory now as she sits
snapping beans and thinking about Raybella Skillen
and how Raybella used to comb her long brown hair;

she'd stand on her front porch combing it out
and the sun would strike it and everyone knew

that every husband wanted to put his hand deep
into Raybella's long brown hair and Raybella knew
and would say things like "Keeping a neat head of hair
is the least you can do for your man," or "The Good Book says
a woman's hair is her crown and glory."

But one day Raybella wouldn't stop combing,
wouldn't go back to her kitchen, her green beans
and salt meat, and they boiled away and burnt
and ruined the pan, and at nine o'clock
she was still combing, and at ten o'clock
women were talking to her, but she just combed
and combed and stared at the sun,
and they had to go get her husband.

"Raybella's gone off the deep end,"
she remembered telling Mr. Skillen
as she snapped another bean now
and thought about how Jesus handled things,
handled them just about the same way she would.

The Comeback of Yma Sumac

El reino muerto vive.—*Neruda*

IN MEMORY OF KARL VON LEUWEN

—————

For decades now her voice, aureate
as Incan gold or the high, hidden cities
of the Andes, lay lost, silenced
by the fad affairs of our fickle ears,
while Yma, in the footsteps of Zog
and Zita, Hapsburgs, and Hohenzollerns, Yma
like some exiled, downcast, once-crowned head, waited
tables or washed the remains of rich sauce
from the plates of men with short memory
and oblivious to wonder, men who could not see
in the polished tines' revealing light
the purple touch and genealogies of grace,
or perhaps Yma simply stared out a window
and watched a world rushing away from the voluptuous days,
but now Xtabay has descended Pentecostal
upon us again and Yma sings in Manhattan
and the crowds begin to remember and roar.

To live in a time freed from history's drift
is solace of sorts. Nothing gone stays gone
forever. The dead return, the forgotten

are recalled, the disgraced revised, washed clean,
their crimes bleached bright and pure: Nixon
turns elder statesman; Pétain, a savior;
Mussolini whispers "Et tu"; and Judas
is canonized—all necessary saints.

History as history was
is all that's finally gone,
and in its tumble down and clutter
we've found the scraps to cloak our dreams.
Everything is missed but disarrayed;
the past is repaved in pyrite, and nostalgia
gated in oyster shell. Everyone is worthy
and every yesterday regretted. History
no longer indicts, for in the terror of the present
is no fear of the past—or any future we might now
in this instant with casual savagery
be hurling into shape.

Cancer Talkers

There are those who love its details,
love them more than the bedroom chronicles
of neighbors and colleagues, whose eyes
widen and glow at the thought
of things big as grapefruits
growing within chests and rectums,
inside friends, movie stars, and even
the anonymous friend of the friend of a friend.
They wonder if the doctors got it all
and talk about the man just eaten up,
the one they just had to sew back together.
They wonder about his wait and whether
he smoked again now that it didn't matter.
They are troubled by bone marrow
and how it's moved, whether it's scooped out
with gleaming surgical spoons
or suctioned into glass tubes, whether
it looks like what they've seen in beef bones.
And they think long on bald women, those
whose hair the hot chemicals loosened from scalps
and whether they went alone
to the wig shop or were accompanied
by a friend who stared or wept. And, of course,
they think of how it would feel
to have a chest smooth as a child's. They talk

of mortgages and insurance, wonder
how the little ones will cope and what she'll do
now or how he'll get along without her.
Their days go by in this talk,
and sometimes at night they even dream of it.
They see it moving within them
like a little ghost, like a child
with a sheet over its head, and they are as frightened
as they were thirty or forty years ago when
that same child stepped from behind a tree
one evening as they walked home
thinking only of mother and dinner.
The ghost child's boo bled their tears
for hours of nights; now, the small swarming cancer
also cries boo, cries beyond recognition, deformed,
gouged out, withered, to a crisp, in cold blood,
and calls for snipers, creatures, nurse killers, and cannibals
to come join him beneath his raging, racing sheet.

Upon Reading in the Newspaper
That a Man in Kentucky Had Cut
Off His Hand and His Foot with
Pocketknives and Then Gouged
Out an Eye in Order That He
Might Go to Heaven

He sat on the sidewalk outside his house
looking at his bloody chunks.
He threw into shrubbery what once
had caressed the hard thighs
of pure and Pentecostal girls.
He kicked at half of what had brought him
to their rooms and trailers. With his one eye
he saw what no longer offended him.
And above his head he felt the air stir
like a rustling of huge birds, and he saw
a golden feather fall, and he knew
that he had been welcomed.
He heard celestial jukeboxes
break forth from the red lips of cherubic girls
voiced in honey and gowned in see-through lace.
And they hard-rocked a stubbed and bloody pain
in the wonder-working power.
And having watched his arm and leg
gush like the garden hose he daily watered
his pole beans and collards with, he, too, knew

the magic and power of blood.
And feeling himself going, he could feel
his shoulder blades begin to grow
and push from his flesh and push with a softness,
a sweetness, a sense of flight.

On a Photograph I Found of
Two Young Factory Workers Standing
beside a Piece of Heavy Machinery
and Inscribed on the Reverse "Sacred
to the Memory of Friendship"

FOR JUSTIN CALDWELL AND ROBERT NIKIRK

Though they did not stand close to each other,
and though they stared from their machine
indifferently, distantly, I do not doubt
they'd known each other's arms and fears.
The mustached one wore a small ring
on his little finger, and neither smiled
as that instant sacred to the memory
was snatched from a factory in Wilson, Kansas,
back when my grandparents were children.
And I saw that the one who'd inscribed it
had pasted on a prescription from F. Zeman, Druggist,
made out for the "Worst Kind of Poison."
And I could imagine how the other
laughed the way friends or wives
laugh at such love-clear jokes.
And I could see him, who, like his friend,
had never read Whitman or Plato or given thought
to the theories of passion, take him
and kiss those quiet lips

and move his hands over his chest and back and thighs
until they both rememorized their love.
And perhaps they rested with a shot of whiskey, a beer,
and talked of the foreman or next Sunday's
lesson on Deuteronomy and what to do
with the extra tomatoes they'd grown,
the talk of those who've come to count
tomorrow assured. And perhaps one said,
"But if we get bad rain this year,
we won't have enough tomatoes to put up."
And the other said, "Maybe you're right;
it'd be a shame not to have enough for winter."
And they talked on like this into days and days
until finally there was nothing:
a house, a cane, an empty bed,
a few jars of juice, a photograph   waiting.

The Correct Answers

to the newspaper's "Christmas Quiz about Europe" should go like this:

1. "A customary Christmas Eve dish in Finland
    is made of . . .
        c) beans and franks."
2. "For hundreds of years, Spaniards
    have followed Christmas Eve mass with . . .
        b) a nationwide slumber party."
3. "A traditional belief throughout Europe is
    that at midnight on Christmas Eve . . .
        d) cows converse."

We are all alike.
Everyone is alike.
Everyone
is always alike:
hope, the bitch slut of history,
repeats the heart,
and we all live out
the old Magi journey.

We sit and wait for the miraculous
as if some grace were our due,
or possible. We eat our beans;
we sleep; we dream
like Europeans on Christmas Eve
and wait the wonders,

hope they will dig themselves
into the time-twisting marrow,
or shower down in angelics
of cash, or simply prolong
the long decay.

It's Christmas Eve
and I am in Arkansas
and will sit down tonight with family and eat;
and perhaps they will pray,
and then I will sleep.
And possibly
when I wake,
something will have happened,
will have descended
like gold or thighs
or even God, and I will be
lifted, lifted
like flaming judgments from hope:
joyed and graced,
calm as the eyes
of a Sienese saint.

The Canticle of End-Times

Assured of the end, of tribulation
and rapture, of the come-round hour,
she rises with the muscle of farmers
stirred by harvest doubts and the length of light.
She rises from a room as simple as the bun of her hair,
as simple as a boiled egg,
simple as lemon juice and warm tap water.
She rises to the fields of sin
as she leaves a room made safe through icon:
above her bed, a young and calling god
come to knock at the heart's door; over her stove the same boy,
nailed, suffocating, beginning the long wait.
And in her purse heavy with salvation
she carries "Words for Modern Man"
arranged in the grammar of fear.
And she stands for hours handing them out,
for hours looking into faces already marked,
for hours reciting the theorems of apocalypse,
the canticle of end-times and the great judging.
And in the evenings when she returns to her room,
her fingers dark with smudged ink,
she washes her hands and sits quietly for a while,
sits looking into the face of the dying boy,
and weeps slow, small tears,
knowing that the beastliness has already begun.

The Kālī Yuga

At the end of the Kālī yuga, the period in
which we are now living, Kālī, the mother
of the universe, will set its destruction into
motion as her consort the Lord of the Dance,
the great god Shiva, in a whirling ring of fire
begins the dance that will destroy the world.

When Buddy Ebsen dies and goes to heaven,
he's going to dance for Jesus,
going to dance an old-time dance
like a hoedown dance danced fast.
An angel may play a jug. And Jesus might
play his fiddle. And Buddy's feet
will tickle the clouds, and he'll dance and dance.
And after the gates are opened to him,
he'll dance down golden streets,
his toes and heels tapping the gold,
and the angel with the jug will follow him,
and so will Jesus. And Buddy will dance
and keep dancing and dance for them all.
And the hard, cold gold will not bruise
his feet for they will be like air,
and Buddy will dance for what would be
hours and hours if watches ran in heaven
and heaven ran on time. And other angels

will find themselves jugs, and archangels
will lay down their horns and pick up fiddles
to play along with Jesus playing for Buddy.
And they will all be happy, and Buddy
will dance on and on till God Himself
takes off His robes, puts on His overalls,
and kicks His feet to dance with Buddy.
And God and Buddy will dance for a day,
a day in which the dance is all,
and God will forget His cranks and gears,
and things will spin till they spin away,
dancing and dancing like Buddy and God.

The Wastes of Resurrection

I'd rather not have to worry with heaven.
—Wilfred Owen, spoken to me in a dream

———————

Heaven's where it's all back
together again, we're told,
where scattered meat and bone
unite to bring some soldier home
to a wife who waited a while,
then remarried, grew old and died.
What bed does God propose
to hold that doubled grief:
to die and wait, then find
that love's forgot—
or does He wed all three
to bed down in polyandry,
then tell the reglued boy,
fifty years maybe sixty, blown
from his desire and thrust, "She's dry,
and her new husband's ass has caved in;
try to make do; a walk might help;
the streets are paved."

Opie and the Apples

When the new kid moved to Mayberry and didn't want to go
fishing with Opie and called him "Dopey" because he said
he'd rather fish than steal apples and Opie asked Andy if
he could fight the new kid because he'd called him names
and Andy said "No" and how that just wouldn't be right neighborly
and how Ope 'u'd just have to find something to like about
the new kid and so Opie stole some apples, too, and got
in trouble and it was a terrible mess and Aunt Bea cried
and cried and Barney wanted to take Opie to the woodshed
but Andy had a big powwow with ol' Ope and Opie just finally
beat the shit out of the new kid who then went fishing with
Opie and decided Aunt Bea, whom he earlier had said looked
like a big-titted warthog, was real pretty and that her
fried chicken was better than anything he ever ate and that
his snooty mother who never fried chicken was a selfish snob
and his father was just too rich and busy to love a little kid,
whose single but very large tear finally made that father see
he needed to take him fishing with Opie and Andy and made
his mother run to Aunt Bea's kitchen begging for her recipe;
so when all that happened on that typical Mayberry day,
I wondered what Andy did when he got horny and if Barney dreamed
of being locked in a cell with Andy and no one would let them out
and there was a big shower nozzle and Andy took lots of showers
'cause he said a man oughta stay clean and Barney felt happy,
happier even than when he patrolled the streets, and if Floyd

ever raised the price of a haircut or nicked an ear, and if
there were high school kids in Mayberry, boys who reached
into the sweaters of girls and girls who ran their hands
over the tight zippers of boys, and if apples ever rotted
in Mayberry, and how loud the preachers got when they talked
of apples and Eve and disobedience and if when Opie learned
to masturbate he would think of this day on which he stole apples
and got in trouble and Aunt Bea cried and cried because she knew
he'd be at himself in a few years and that socks and sheets
would show his shame and there would be nothing,
nothing she could say to him and that pimples would rise
on his face and that he would find his hand in sweaters
and his tongue deep into the cleft of the world's imperfections.
And she wept and tore chunks from her hair
and gnawed her knuckles knowing there was not grace enough
even here, even in Mayberry, to seal the thighs of Eve.

Jam

The farmer's wicked wife does not put
cracklings in the farmer's corn bread.
At night she does not ask him
if he wants to use her.
She's never cleaned out the cistern,
and she often puts eggs in the icebox
that she's not wiped off.
The farmer begs for children;
his wife giggles silently.
And under the brown canvas of revivals,
the Holy Spirit moves her pelvis and tongue
with the eating fire of quicklime.
And the other wives listen
as her egg-smooth lusts are confessed
and forgiven. Her testimonies to their husbands'
abilities with tractors and ropes, the breaking
of sod tight as their muscles
do not please them. They do not please
her sweating husband, whose lips
twitch into smiles that are not smiles.
Though the revival man
who lays on the hands quivers for her confessions
and her hot bread and jams, her thick white hominy
and breaded steaks. And in his unknown voice
which she alone understands and moves her tongue to,

he begs for more in the name of Jesus, sweet Jesus.
And the daily read and curling pages
of her husband's Bible are thumbed
in the sweat of fear. And the wives sweat
in the sweat of fear and think they hear
the sound of wasps. But their slim husbands
sitting in open-necked shirts
only watch her God-touched hips
and feel breezes blowing through the rapture-rank tent.

How I Tried to Explain
the Certainties of Faith and
Petrunkevitch's Famous Essay
on the Wasp and the Tarantula
to a Pentecostal Student Worried
about My Soul

He told me how he'd prayed,
besought God with Habakkuk's fervor,
and how into those prayers I
like some prodigal had come
and stood in their heart
naked and ignorant, wobbling
on a rapturous balance
unaware, blind to the hand
and script which declared me
weighed and wanting, deaf
to the timbrels of angels
gliding as if they were rounding
again and again a gold and glowing rink.
Then Jesus, blonder now than ever,
his robe open slightly, his pectorals
hard as hatchets, his thighs
glistening, appeared saying,
"That man dreams of whores
and hacking them up. Go ask
after his soul." And so, he'd come,

but now wept and bit at his hands,
reached across the desk, took my hand
and kissed me, pressing hard his tongue.

Still holding his hand, I told him
my soul was well, that I would hack
no one, and had little use for visions,
but that Christ worked the world
like a wasp, worked it in a catching
and planting; that the sting, the seeding,
the final devouring *was* the Jesus-journey,
the whole point, the point of anything—
the point of inexplicable need
or the commands of a glistening god—
and the price, the price
even pagans pay, the price
to charge away profane uncertainty.

About Their Father's Business

For he is of the tribe of Tiger.
—from "Jubilate Agno"

---

1. DISCOVERIES

It was not Brendan's hand that drove the oar
or held the helm, not Brendan's eyes
that mapped his way, nor Brendan's prayer
that blessed the sea's great gleaming subtleties.

No ordinary thing set him
to strike the ogham onto stones
and cross and bless the new world's rim
or take the savage in his arms.

At the red pivot of his heart
the Christ-lion crouched and spun,
purred round love's axised torque
and compassed him till it was done.

2. VISIONS

As Louis Wain's madness grew, his art became
increasingly inspired. Santa cats held small haloed
tabbies before wise cats bearing gifts, while others
grew so bright and geometric, their fur so dazzling,
they were indistinguishable from light.

He dreamed the Second Coming, dreamed it
quickened with cottonwood and come too soon,
dreamed it finally flung to an ink pot's lip—
a weight, a ball, a pen point's shimmering.

And he awoke in anger's sweat
to tell us how the fetus held
until it drank its weight of blustered blab
and then went out.

And on that same thorn-dazzled day,
crouched at anger's sullen shrine,
he saw what prowls the festered air
and holds the storm's still silent eye:

the quivering haunches' burnished blur, the spring,
the leap, the incandescent fur.

3. QUESTIONS

Did Curly really die because Larry
and Moe hit him in the head so much?
Did something happen backstage one night
at the Mickey Mouse Club?
Why do comic strips exist?
Who eats Spam?

Oh, if I could only know the answers,
I'd slip into the long, rare robes
of the Magus, and as Sirius rose

with the sun, I'd blend honey
with chokeberry and mercury.
I'd refine plasters, distill the draughts,
and administer them as balm and wine,
having come round to the knowledge
of important things, the knowledge
of what offends me, is maggot to me.

The bald head was slapped so much,
I heard that it caved in one day,
and Curly stumbled as Larry and Moe
jumped up and down. And I heard
that in the studio one night
behind the big mouse head,
a certain man—old, mustached—
lifted her sweater and hugged her
until she said, "If you're gentle."
And someone told me that Spam
went well with eggs
and B. O. Plenty, Terry, and Abner, and all of them
on Sunday mornings before church,
that it even tasted like the corned beef
Jiggs always dreamed Maggie might let him have.

This is what I have been told,
but I am wandless and robeless,
unable to kill or redeem you,
being neither lion, star, nor mage.

But you should know
that I have heard a rustling in the night,
the slow stalk of massive paws,
and smelled musk's high anger on the air.

Expulsions

. . . in the nineteenth century backwoods
farmers in the U.S.A. digging up a thighbone
taller than a man feared they had found
the bones of the fallen angels.
—Nancy Newhall

He often thought of them,
those storms of flaming trash
falling
back in that turning world
before the land was done,
thought of them and feared
the humor of his God,
feared He might be fat,
feared He laughed,
that He laughed
like a fat boy with firecrackers,
that Adam, wingless now
and always falling, was the joke—
monkey lust in angel grace—
and that we too were shaped
for ruin, ordained
for danger, for dark curves.

And on his tongue he smelled
the stench of wings

wrathed to pitch. He wept
at what he furrowed out:
teeth like fists,
great pelvic shards, coal
that once held thighs
curved with risks.

And he'd cut wings
on planks for markers
and put them there and there
and there till the fields failed
and he forgot his fears—
of birds, of locusts, of thick grubs
glowing at the roots, curving
them like thumbs, and even
the talk of neighbors, and even
a neighbor's tongue in the mouth
of his wife and down and along
the curves of his wife,

because the fields were sanctified,
made holy by his hand. And he
in glittering arrogance arose
and went out, redug
the smoothest bone and lay down
beside it, watched it
finally now and at last
flesh out.

And he was down and in love,
and it was like Babylon,
tiered gardens and the smell
of cedar, of curves and danger.
And he lay there copulating
with the air until the noise
of the wolves grew louder
than the thoughts he could think,
louder than her splendid sighs.

Baptisms

When he spoke of revelations,
his voice covered her
like anointings, and she knew things,
knew God was in his tongue,
on his lips, shining
on the gold, and way down
where sound started, knew
he was right, like before,
like when he said
she wouldn't bleed
when her mole came off,
Jesus having already bled
the afflictions of organs
out, the sins of the flock
out, and how her blood
was cleansed of cancers, cleansed
before she was even born,
cleansed in Judea
when the veil was rent.
And she remembered his fingers
in the hair under her arm
and how he felt the mole, how
when he rolled it back
and forth between his thumb
and forefinger, rolled it slowly,

whispering "Jesus Jesus," she
had to take deep breaths.
And she wished for a talent,
for something special she could do,
like tool his name in Old English
to the back of a belt.
And especially now because
he was right, because
God was all over him, because
when he was close and down
in your face praying, you could smell
his breath, and it was like bread,
and he was saying heaven would be withheld
from those baptized in water alone,
for where were the nails,
the Judas baptism of iron,
and where was the spoiling fire
of harrowed hell's cleansing.
And she knew he was right.
And on Monday she went out
and bought nails and dynamite
and filled her car, and she thought
of him and of Jesus, of the pig iron
and flames, and she remembered Jesus saying
to suffer the children, and then
she was sure she was sure,
and it was like rainbows arcing,
and she was on her way.

Conversions

*Well, my marriage finally did fall apart and I lost the
house, but I am really happy now; it all led me to Him.
John, believe me, He's the real sweetness and light.*

———————————

I've seen a crippled lust prod men
toward Christ with the fire they could not make,
heard the tabernacles of hysteria shake and timbrel forth
the things the flesh would not release,
smelled sin glow bright as halos in the scalps' grease,
and watched the spittled foam
bead at the praising, stuttered edges of speech,
until smoldering in the impotent auras of despair, they were at last
consumed. I've watched the bolted embrace of marriage
rust over and disengage in a sharding down, and seen them then
rise, but to no more than a wafer's reach. And I've stared
at the lunatics whipped and dancing their rapturous hosannas,
their eyes luxurious with tears, with the ecstatic fruit
of thorn and nail.

It is impossible not to notice, impossible
to avert the eyes where frenzy spins
and whole congregations run leaping before you
like plagues, brown and biblical.

But who can say I'd not be as touched and springing,
my sight as furiously gazed, my tongue as thick and gabbled,
were I to lose my son, and this flesh of mine empty out all joy.
The skin of even me, then, might be animated
by where despair had pushed so far, might be quickened and convulsed.

I wished him well but prayed
for calm repose and empty sky,
that I might never know
the whirling psalms of such peace,
his starred and honeyed bliss.

Theological Meditation

At the heart of the wood
lie only the loins' sweet shudder
and a wide white sleep,
smooth and polished as glazed snow.

And for no more than that
we fret and flame,
risk the body's wreck
and the mind's fire going:
all to mumble our greed toward . . .

what? an emptiness
shaped like our own confounding flesh;
or worse, some deified orifice,
a function of blood and muscle,
the residue of instinct
left piled and steaming
at the cave's back
deep in Neanderthal dark?

But were the mystery solved
and all saw the plotless pages,
the million picaresque years,
would any ring of men then dance
in supple time, lift voice in chant,
or frame ritual from frenzy,

or would the rhythms rise
flush and foaming to rally
old enmity and the groin's random temper
to new purpose—certain this time, sanguine, and malign?

Silage

The way she wore sweaters
and brushed her hair
made all the boys wish
she'd play strip poker
and dance like the woman
who came to the fair each fall
and undid those fresh boys
still dreaming of damp middle fingers
and barns filled with hay and dollars,
undid their stiff fathers
away from wives and tired
of thick-boned women who smelled
like bacon and sweat, undid
their thick mothers tired of prized cakes
and quilts, of jars of perfect jam, of "yes,"
and undid their wheezing grandfathers
fogged over by angina and age,
old men grinning as the past
stirred again in their laps.

Jesus, the things she did to those boys
when she wore sweaters and did her hair like that!
When they slept, they thought of her
naked and limp, her muscles turned
to mud, thought of themselves over her

giggling like their grandfathers;
thought of rich barns and kitchens,
the denseness of corn,
thick acres with ears bursting open
spilling dimes into their pockets;
thought of crops they'd harvest
as easily as girls. And breasts
and thighs, damp deep triangles of hair,
bright pails of cream, and hooves
thick with glue, whole boxcars
of marbled meat, and fat as white
as milk flowed in and out of their sleep,
blending and rising
like the rank, rich silage
they could always smell,
they could always taste
on the backs of their teeth.

Shitheads

Their hardiness comes without effort,
as easily as salvation swarms
out of men who've heard their names
cried from clouds. But it's the urgency
of their need one most notices, how
from their furious grips and wide, white smiles,
their eyes leech to yours, and their voices,
warm and as smeared with vibrato as a preacher's,
swoop over you like a fumbling lover,
and you are mauled by their appetites,
their measured dreams and confessions,
hopes shaped from the architecture of excess.

These men know where they are going,
and they insist their futures upon you, beg you
to smile back in mirrored vacancy the same smile
that sits on their faces, clean and neat as their rectums.
And knowing the paving will soon turn
to gold and their speed will increase again and again,
knowing it's all close enough to smell,
they scramble for the things they will need:
carphone, Rolex, deodorant. They buy up the secrets
of success: a Masonic handshake, a Rotarian luncheon,
the arcana of wine or futures, the vocabulary of ease;
and as they rise, they slough off the roles they've outgrown

like old skins or embarrassments. There's no goal
but ascension. And they know that God's floating eye
on the backs of dollars looks down on their work,
approves and blesses them.

Sometimes if you are lucky, you can glimpse them
as they pass, can hear their voices
trailing like crepe streamers.
But at such swarming speeds, they're pitched too high
to catch; are indistinct as pond spawn;
are like the cold rushing syllables I hear
each winter mazing the webbed pockets of my walls.

Reflections on the
Progress of the Western
Intellectual Tradition
from Thales to Crick
and Watson

I. THE MYSTERY

My hands have held
apples, and my fingers
slipped the pure curve
of pears as they have
slipped through lace
and linen to circuit
the curves of love
with no thought of why,
with no thought
of lust's cool compass
or the blind geometries
of desire.

2. THE COMEDY

If thinking does existence prove,
I must beware of crowds and eyes;
for if I think too long on love,
private proofs materialize.

We dream of spiraling spells
down the twined helices of the heart.
But the heart is out of plumb. Fine tools
cannot survey its slant—nor even art
align what's long lain at the bestial point.

Hunting for a New Chairman; Thinking about Giotto

Even the old ones puffed with uric acid
and swollen feet attempt a briskness
now that joy comets down close. They spin
like bits of dirt and lint tumbling in the sunlight
through these corridors of hope and dream.
They speak and smile again, and though it's eight
do not smell of last night's ease. No bourbon's needed
to whiskey dreams these waiting weeks,
for they're drunk on new space, a place
where files bright as this year's dimes
bulge with the secrets that have obsessed whole years:
why Professor X resigned or what the cheerleader
really said about Professor Y and on and on.
Their tongues begin to taste again and wander the room
that smells of new shoe leather and smaller mortgages,
a room spinning as securely as a chairman's clock
ticking the fat, tenured years into gentle sloth.
They dream the hopes of mazed rats,
and all joy rests in the right turn, the move
that leads to cheese and whole semesters of sleep,
to things that are for them like starlight
and the music of spinning moons, girls in gossamer
so thin no guessing's necessary, or a chapel
in Padua, for example, where stars once fell
to a man's moving hand, where wonders began.

Locomotion and Starlight

The light was cool as it drifted
down into my grandmother's garden,
into the stalks of corn,
the blades and pods of garlic.
Under such stars old men
thinking only of pensions and biscuits,
the cinders they've survived,
have slumped over, gone out like wet fusees;
firemen have lost count of coal
and huge wheels have slowed;
smiling call boys
punctual with dispatches
and the rousing of brakemen
have dreamed the dreams
of a drunk at the switch.
Though my grandmother said,
Certain signs are good for crops.
And the man next door who used to fire
but now made medicine said,
The garlic's ready to be ground.
And a call boy said, *In a month
I'll be switching.* And the light frolicked
through my grandmother's dark pantry,
fingered the jars of salves and preserves,
invaded the suppers of her lodge,

climbed the trellises, hammered hydrangeas,
and strutted to the turkey
as if it were a shape, a thing, an invited guest.

Dreams of Standing

The retarded boy
thumbed the art book
and twisted his head
with the resolve
of a bug's head twisting
toward food, and stared
as if his eyes were
lidless bulges. Then
he spread his legs there
on the floor of the bookshop
where the breasts,
the uncluttered pubis, the dense
wood, the apples, the thick coils—
soft, scaleless,
like a fat woman's arm
widening in its heavy rise—
shimmered him. And it was like
riding, like the grinding spin
of his great tricycle's wheels,
that slight pressure at his anus,
his legs firing like shouts
to piston the miles, working
as they worked in dreams of standing
near them, their faces just
beginning to pimple, sullen,

pouting at their virginity,
and smelling of ripenings:
crusted cheeses, clean laundry
flapping in the bright cold.
And the boy would sweat
in those dreams like these
sweated him now. But in bed
and in the thickness of his dream,
he could focus his tongue to twist
his eyes awake and rise and ease the dream,
but here on the floor of the bookshop,
unfocused, alone with Eve
and awake, his lips drying,
beginning to crust and glisten
like snailwork, there was
no salvaging, no salvaging
of himself at all.

The Myths of Meanness

And then he chewed her whole breast off,
or so my grandmother told me
and whispered to me of meanness
as she recounted dark details
that she and certain frightened friends
alone knew all about, but which,
of course, and wisely so, were hushed,
for *they* dared not and would not had they dared
declare to widows and virgins
the details of meanness.
And she said, *there's a lot
of meanness going around now.*
And I told her that I did not believe
her story, that I'd heard the same story
before and in other places and that
if she could remember, she too
would recall it. It was the same,
except that it was always told,
depending on where it was told,
about a Black or Indian or Chinaman.

And I thought of all the myths of meanness:
those gleaming silver hooks
left dangling from car doors
when cars in just the lucky nick
pulled away from down the petting lanes;

or the tiny black widows burrowed in
those stiff, unwashed, and daily sprayed bouffants,
black widows with hourglasses as red
as what those girls had planned to give
for beer, for football boys, and even love
later that special night,
hourglasses counting away
all the pretty prom queens' final dances;
or finally, wrapped in a shimmer of evil,
the crying girl who begs a ride
from beside some bashed car and what was once
her sweet-tongued boy,
only at her sad father's door to leave
and leave a sad father weeping
over a twenty-year-dead girl
and leave the countless and perplexed drivers
dark roads to follow home.

It was a white man that did it,
she quickly said, sure now
she had a new story
and that the meanness was confirmed.

And all the old women
amid their rows of beets,
their fear of cheese, their furious sewing,
worried over the final days.

Bees

In my father's catalpa,
deep in dead limbs,
was the tiny growl of bees.
Saps had stilled and grown silent;
only the humming of bees
remained to rise
through the branches
where once green and freshness rose.
Now droned songs alone
pushed from moldy hollows,
small siroccos
stirred by the swinging
of rusty wings.

I have seen the greed of bees
hanging on small fuzzed feet
as dense puffs of pollen
or heavy, heavy globes of nectar
pulling the legs
until they were like plumb bobs
in that bright quiet of afternoon
when gathering is solitary
and children's eyes are closed
and their ears silent
to the drone and friction
of thighs.

My mother ordered
the hooded men
who came with their nets
and boxes of fresh comb
and fire to smoke the bees,
but they swarmed
and it was like blood hovering in the air
and the tree was burned.
And I still remember the final spindles of smoke
and my father beside me
running his fingers through his ashen hair.

Remembering My Father Riding

Though I was still a child,
I remember him (already too old
for such showings off) wobbling,
smiling, waving from the bike
as he circled the grape arbor
and rode between the tomatoes and peas,
smiling and waving, and me
crying, "Daddy, Daddy, stop."
I could see his feet slipping,
the wobbling bike going down,
and him falling into the garden,
into the tomatoes, their stakes
hitting his face, his glasses shattering,
could see him lying still,
the bicycle wheels still turning,
and dust rising and glistening in the sun.
And I called and called to him,
but he just kept riding,
kept circling the arbor
through the tomatoes and peas,
kept circling and smiling,
circling and circling the garden,
and smiling and waving
and smiling and waving.

Elegiac Stanza on a Photograph of Ethel Rosenberg in Her Kitchen

It sits on top my desk, but it is faced
So that the sun will not cause it to fade:
The photographs we save are like the taste
Of honey on a sharpened razor blade.

Elegy

It has already been observed that being an American
is difficult. I reobserve, renote the fact: it is
difficult. And I don't know what to do about it.
I think it has been this way for some time now,
a long time in fact, though the last ten years
have seemed, how shall I put it, "memorably difficult"?
And these last few days? They have been very hard.
It's as if blood had dried on me, and when I move,
it flakes and falls, and these reminders drop around me.
I see them at my feet. And I despair. I say things like
"It's not my fault; please don't blame me," or "I'm
nobody." To no avail. Excuses are useless.
Salvador Allende was murdered in Santiago, Chile,
two days ago. Excuses are useless. "I'm nobody."
Four U.S. battleships were positioned
off Chile's coast. Excuses are useless. Reminders
drop around me. I think they are shaping into words
I can't read. I know what they are spelling. I apologize.
"But you've got to understand I'm nobody." I lie
and say I'm from Canada. Excuses are useless.
Salvador Allende was murdered in Santiago, Chile,
and I despair. The White House has still made no
comment. Excuses are useless. I reobserve, renote,
and despair. To no avail. "And what if I were
an American; what could I do? I'm nobody.

I'm not the President." Excuses are useless.
"Not guilty, not guilty," I insist. To no avail.
Salvador Allende was murdered in Santiago, Chile,
and I despair. Excuses are useless. Allende is dead.
I despair. To no avail. Allende is dead. It is difficult.

Elegy in September

FOR MAO

Though golden carp still flash and swim
and wheat is sickled and brought down,
though plums are still to prune and trim,
the central man is gone.

Elegiac Ode

Stop and lament over the grave of Kroisos, whom furious
Aries destroyed one day as he fought in the front ranks.
—inscription on a kouros figure, circa 520 B.C., *Athens*

He stands and smiles a smile to stun our sight.
His Attic lips reveal antiquity's disdain
   For all the centuries to come, the blight
Of brutish air, a blighted future's trashed terrain.

Could Delphic voices turn and laurel his lips again to song,
     I'd have them chorus on and on.

   But now it is for Kroisos I lament,
Whose smile of certain logic Aries kissed one day,
   Though still his supple beauty is unspent
As when his lips were poised in pure tranquility.

Could classic song return and animate his scattered dust,
     We'd pray him back from Aries' lust.

   Excess has driven its barbaric weight
Through near a million days since Kroisos stepped from stone.
   Could gold and Grecian mean now tolerate
The measures of intemperate time, an age of bone?

Could Kroisos stand and rise to song, his lips would still remain
     Fixed in perpetual disdain.

Babies on the Beach

To call their presence incongruity
is to say nothing about them, nothing
about them as a unit, plump and naked,
ignorant of cadence, moving like clouds
across the sand, their brows bent
in obvious and resigned anger at the tasks
before them, at the immensities presented
by beach and sun, by sand and drifts
of uncountable shells split from their pairs,
smaller than their fingertips, anonymous
and unnameable even had they desire
and all of time to sit and choose them names,
and as clean as the sea leaves the long wrecked.
But what of their weapons? The claws
of washed-out crabs, the blade shards of conch,
driftwood, and weed for rope. But most
their tiny wills which melt and cast the lead,
cast casing for what the will has mined.
But what is that will, and why is it set
among metals, nitre, and sulphur?
And what is it determined in the presence
of those unnavigable immensities to chart?
Is it set against the fathers and mothers
fled from the beach, for weeks at least now gone,

gone long enough for them to perceive
desertion and then community, and later to arm,
to weld their wills to a single urge?

Large birds circle the shore; big fish
eye the land; these babies can't go on for long.
Wrath's brittle diet fragiles the freshest bone,
and soon in a great swooping and lunging,
they will all be taken like tiny wrecks,
up and out and back again, one
with the immense, the anonymous, the clean.

Flowers for Robert Mapplethorpe

I.

Near the Pantheon
a boy whose shoulder shows
the purple of desire,
whose muscled chest
is brown as dying callas,
offers the tourists flowers
and expensive chestnuts
out of season.

His jeans are as tight
as the unblossomed peonies
I think of buying. I ask him
how long before they open.
"Tomorrow," he lies. Still
I take bundles back
and chestnuts, too. Tonight
he and his leathered
bullyboy will think of me
when they buy wine and Vaseline,
will think I am waiting
tomorrow's hard buds to open
as I sleep, will think
I'll awaken in a kind of tourist's rage
with what the night has made.

2.

There are always flowers left
on the grave of John Keats.
Neat schoolboys in blazers
leave the roses they bought
on the Spanish Steps. And they
go home to England intending
to think, henceforth,
on beauty alone, and always
tell the truth. Thick ladies
in suits come to lay violets
there. They hand new cameras
to strangers who blur them
but save for a fall's coming class
some proof of love, some sketching
of why their eyes glaze so
when they speak of him, glaze
like sex or preaching,
to prove a love
they've forced for years indifferent teens
to learn like prayers.
                        Some will recall
an urn, a bird, a silent peak,
a blurred, bending figure placing violets
once when they were young, their skin
quick as matches, when they hated
school and Keats and anything that held

the eyes, the tongue, the hands
from love's circuit, those gaudy explorations
older, richer than the oldest poems.

3.

Wheat and poppies bloom
along the Appian Way.
Bees have built
into the broken walls,
and honey slips down
the bricks.
A motorcycle passes.
The sound is mean as bees,
angry as a hundred hives.
The boy in rear holds
the hips of his friend
tightly, and they both are
laughing as if the comb of the world
was dense, was full, was theirs.

4.

Crossing the Ponte San' Angelo,
I see a page ripped from a magazine.
A penis is poised for entry
from behind. A long-haired girl
looks over her shoulder and speaks.
In a balloon over her head the words

are written out. She says, "Stick it in."
Bernini's statues look down.
Hadrian's tomb rises in front.
A man carrying roses and bread
passes me, also notices the page.
"There's nothing you'd want there,"
he says. He is younger than I,
looks neither prude nor lunatic,
but is wrong. Had I enough Italian,
I'd tell him no, that I want
the mean words of their rough love,
that I would take them and make silent
as the rise of bread their copulation,
that I would press them like roses
or fold them like a friend's handkerchief
stiffened with the crust of need.

Coda

The bruised boy found leather
for his labor, and the bikers
alone where poppies bloom
saw honey break from a wall.

But those leaden virgins in love with Keats,
the boy bringing home bread and roses
only found ritual at the petals' lips—and shadows,
the shades of lusts embraced in sleep alone.

The Mysteries: Elegy at Century's Close

IN MEMORY OF FREDDIE MERCURY

I. THE SYMBOL

Moments before you might notice the glove,
her face would hold your gaze until
her nipples radiant beneath the lace
took your eyes in a dazzling of copper,
and in a kind of shame at the discovery,
the theft, your eyes would drop to the white glove
held as she might hold some animal, limp,
drugged, and you would stare at the folded glove
white and wounded, but radiant in glories
of abundance, soft at the prism's thrill
where colors in vibrating conjunction
separate to fall into cold order.
And it demanded ecstasy, magic,
demanded all philosophy's closure
and the slow aphrodisia of praise,
a praise whole thrusting days were required
to raise. And then the glove slipped from her hand.

You thought to pick up the glove, to return
to her hand this thing that out-thrilled her face
and all the soft wealth of her breasts,

but it was gone. And not until later
on the frozen pond did you see it
as tartan mufflers snapped the air
and skates knifed along ice as hard and grey
as winter's hanging sky. The air
itself seemed cast in grey, and snow began
to fleck the air and fall on skaters there
spinning in circles on the ice in grey
winter's perfect afternoon's cold cold air.
And on thick grey ice lay the glove burning
while oblivious boys skimmed past the balanced
girls a-twirl as snow scattered in their hair,
swift, silent, past the glowing glove aware
only of friction, and the pond's rapid return.

Near the old bakery, now a powdered ruin—
though the air still seemed to hold the odor
of seedcakes and high-risen loaves—the glove
lay in a stubble of dry grass, lay there
like softest flesh in a cradle of hair,
like something of porcelain and pearl.
And around it stood a crowd of men
staring. And you, too, were there staring,
frightened someone might reach into the grass
and take the glove before you could say,
"I've long sought . . ."

2. THE OFFERING

Oh, we've always known
where love's tent was pitched.
There are no surprises down there,
down in the warm and yeasty dark.
But in the face! No one had looked
into love's Janused frame before,
into the death's-head smiling there,
and seen the eyes milky with memory's loss
barely holding their socket's space
while the breath molded over
and the cheeks fell to the bones' frame.

That love has come to exact such tribute
fouls its history. And even mystery's realm
withers smaller still:

Heaven-striding stars shaping to flesh;
or the rapturing, plentied fields of grain;
light sickled down in the wheelings of ripe flame;
and wine poured from water; or elegance from gabble
have all bowed to fact.
                              Now carbon unveils
the mystery and electrons unmask the myth;
and even we are unraveled
at some swollen, erogenous *I*
where we squat and cringe,
grunting and grabbing.

And love, too, is mocked,
for it was love that took them,
not easy passion, not the labyrinths of lust;

even if his name's unknown, his lips
and body's pressure forgotten, the taste
of sweat lost with other tastes and other times,
need, regardless of its geographies,
is still love's *other* name: distinct, clear,
and pure as a patronym.

3. THE ORACLE

See them, those fleet of foot wending their way
through the grove in cadenced footfall, moving
like figures in a frieze—bright-robed Bacchae
or glistening athletes. Yet see these proving
by their motions that it's not ecstasy
they seek nor any Delphic mystery.

The busloads come because they've heard they should,
not for words once poured pure as springwater
from the laureled lips of Pythia. She stood
where now slouches a droning tour leader.
Cameras go off, snap the scene randomly,
frame it in thin rectangular memory.

The world's ruined center mirrors now the heart's:
no longer does Doric discipline define

or tolerance mold discourse or the arts
to question our measure and design.
No oracles rise in blessings to ease
these days, days only fit for elegies.

For a Friend Whose Son Committed Suicide

There aren't any words to help us live.
The days treat us like drunken husbands.
   Living demands we give
up everything we loved, and it hands
into our hands dirt, boxes of dirt,
   rooms of dirt, houses, whole houses
   of dirt. Though always at the start,
we think we hear other promises.

There are not any words to help us
when deaths and the other desertions
   come whacking and then leave us
lessened in their long divisions.
There is no act to perform against it.
   We weep until we stop.
   The quotient of loss is a wind
that blows memories away. It tastes like dirt.

Thinking of Maria Theresa Broussard, a Pregnant Girl in My Freshman Class My First Semester in Louisiana

I am here at an end tip of things.
The Gulf curls in a few miles away,
and she comes to my office daily.
One is cautious of the weather here.
I'm told alligators are sleeping
in the mud only a few miles away.
I'm shown bottles of huge green pills
she takes for things I've forgotten.
Her mother and sisters are sad,
though the wisteria has been like
music this year, and the camellias
as tight as confectioners' roses.
She tells me about the boy and how he . . .
Since I've been here, I've bought chances
on nine church-sponsored raffles sold me
in front of Kroger's on Saturdays.
Aphids are lush here, and I've learned
the proper proportions of poisons
and oilicides. And my wife's garden
has sprung from the wet dirt like babies.
In my office she shows me pictures
she's drawn: mice holding floppy flowers,
faceless children in antique bonnets.

She promises me a phoenix.
I smile and ask her how she's doing.
She twists her arms and shows me she is
double-jointed. A friend is giving her
a CB radio. "It will help,"
she tells me. There are large green palms here,
and I think of their white hearts, but we
no longer import them from Brazil,
or so the man at Kroger's tells me.
"This is the end," he tells me. And so
I take them all. And she smiles at me
because it will help, and I ask her
what CB name she'll take for herself.
"Sophisticated Lady," she says.
She says, "Lots of people call me that."
"That's nice," I say. She brought me three bells
for my window, and I hung them there.
I've not asked what she'll name her child.
It will be born on her birthday,
she says. The Gulf curls in.
The wind has not moved the bells.

Seeing a Girl Who Looked
like a Well-Known Child Actress
Walking toward San Tomé, the
Church in Toledo Where El Greco's
Burial of the Count of Orgaz
Hangs

———————

As dark and temptingly grown
and with the same eyes, the same
soft but near-masculine head,
the same thick brows, and
with the same magical breasts
they both understood, she wandered
toward San Tomé and the *Burial of Orgaz.*
She paused at a cafe and the corduroyed boys
to see herself barely quiver in their stares,
barely come back
like a figure before a mirror
whose silver has slipped.
Too caught in themselves, their smokes and talk,
they hardly noticed the eyes, the head,
the brows, or even those breasts
they'd soon work days and spend days of work to taste.
And so she turned toward San Tomé, turned
toward the painting, and I watched her turn,
watched her move toward the doors,

saw her hand go out,
and I wanted to shout,
"Yes, yes, I understand."

But in moments she would be before it,
amid Japanese and nuns and tourists from Louisiana,
before it, before the dark face of the dead count,
before the dark and dying faces that surrounded him.
And she would see that though angels filled the air,
the bent body of Orgaz did not ascend,
that though Japanese and nuns and tourists from Louisiana
had come to a church, no hymns were on their lips,
no hands shook hallelujahs above their heads,
no tongues stuttered incomprehensibles of the New Jerusalem.
For here El Greco crowded out Christ, crowded him
with the dark, bent body of Orgaz and a grey dying
that pushed from under the doors, that ran
like soured honey down the alleys of Toledo, that rose
into the sky above Toledo and out and out and out.

And one who had seen the grey face of Orgaz
in his own, who'd taken his share of soured sweets
put his back to the painting
and moved in front of the girl
and stared at her breasts, stared
with such ripe and burgeoning prophecy
she turned from him and from Orgaz,
turned out the doors and back up the streets, back

to the cafe where again she looked
but only for the length of a laugh
and a quick toss of her long hair as she turned,
turned into the now clean, now free and honeyed streets of Toledo.

Here in Louisiana

Here in Louisiana it is December now.
The eaves are free and even. The blank sky hangs here
and seems to wait. Late bananas
are beginning to turn, may even be
ready before the frost stops their sweetening.
Still, this weather winters a few leaves brown,
drives some birds still further south,
and forces roaches beneath the loose bark of live oaks
or deep into the fronds of palms, under old planks
or here and there in the warmer dark.

Today I realized I'd not seen one in weeks.
We live with them here, with their presumption
and prowls, casually, as casually
as we live with humidity and small craft warnings,
with our governors and hurricanes.
They don't distress us quite like they
distress others. And our complaints are resigned,
informal, furyless. Such small, quick acts of God
racing out over kitchen counters
are too fast for more concern—or swatters, usually.

Cracked, they stir more disgust than let alone
to romp over cake crumbs and clean plates:
being big as thumbs,
broken, such things spill their creamy thickness

like salves or clots or rancid lotions.
And unless ground to grease,
some brown fragment will twitch for a day or more
till others clean the carapace to pristine silence.

And so we usually leave them alone,
wait on winter to pretty our kitchens,
forget them till spring, till camellias return
and wisteria twines the fences of south Louisiana,
covers clotheslines, the backs of greenhouses and garages,
drifts over bayous and fields and out toward the Gulf,
the waves and spray, till on fragrant, rainless evenings
out on walks we hear a stirring, what seems at first a fine,
faint mist striking the scattered leaves.

The Surrounding Grace

I've nothing clever to say
about this
most ordinary of events,
a progress
common as desire.

Had some strange, bright wish,
the kind that fames out
one's wit and name, occurred,
I'd have wished it
for this flesh
fragile as a yolk,
these bones
finer than a quail's.

But none did, and so
I find the wish I wish
in a cliché, the third of a cliché,
the dullest prose: I hope
my child will be healthy.
Money I can give it,
and happiness finally
is always singular.

I'm nearly forty, though,
accustomed to myself,
to wife, work, and the stuff
of routine. And now
to let swim into my address
and concern a thing
to worry up whole years,
decades, the rest
of what I've got
is need's strangest
quirking of me yet.

Time, that soil of lust,
of greed's multiplication,
may set us apart, wither
love down, and make you dream
of other fathers, other names.
But I'd have you difficult
and dark, as hateful
as my parents said I was,
to having you sweet
and slow, unable to catch
the strange, bitter grace
you soon will enter into.

A Crown of Promise

FOR DAFYDD

———————

I. POEM CONCLUDING WITH A LINE FROM EURIPIDES

My son restores what time has taken.
The past is gathered up full-fleshed,
incarnadined now whole and hallowed,
returned in processions from the soured stone and mold.
And this is rapture,
time's fullness in aureate blossom,
the kingdom and promise of pearl. My father and grandmother
rise, and my mother is elixired back
into her agile joy. The air is pungent
with pear, with lemon yeast,
and the goods of gardens.
And nothing but anger is alien as he
or is it I lie in the quilts
of our parents' great bed,
complete, singing, and oblivious
to the bones of fear.
O God, Beast, Mystery, come.

II. THE THINGS I WOULD TELL MY SON OF GODS, BEASTS, AND MYSTERY

Be in no hurry to find them.
Let them seek you if they will.
Their sport is play,
and there is always time.
No fires wait the loiterer,
no blackened angelic grotesques,
no lack of joy. Trust this
as you would the strength of my arms,
as you would your mother's love, and know
a sure crazing will claim the eyes
and atomize the sight,
will stun down to gabble
the tongues of those who intrude
the sacred wood. Whole lives,
complete and wholly blest, can pass
without mystery. Life's gift comes
with no demands, and love alone
is all the duty we need know.

III. THE DUTY OF LOVE

When I am shadow stuff again
and vague as my mother's dream of me
before my birth, alive only
in the communion of ancestors,

in the unshakable chemistry at the depth
of your cells, or arcing in the fire
of your brain, or rippling outward
in some perpetuating kindness of my hand—
or cruelty or accident—
and when your mother, too, has grown vague,
her voice unrecallable, her face
clear and exact only in snapshot,
only on old vacations or the starts of school,
on birthdays as blown from your memory
as past wishes, the days
she and I could not bear to leave or let
to memory's thoughtless slide,
then see us in some face
you've come to hate,
or having fled those traps of fear,
in eyes you'd not think ours, lips
you'd not wish on yours. See us there, Dafydd,
there alone, whole and restored.

In Primary Light

FOR CAROL

In Maine's broad and bronzing light—
in lemon pungence, brazen
and honeyed, full as wheat and amber's
wide ranging—in such light spangling down
along its bouldered shore,
its water-shined and barnacled stone
my son and I climbed hand in hand
and watched between quick tides
the minerals' flicker beneath the Atlantic's
thin receding, the stones' lightening dry
before a wet hand or returning tide
caressed berylliums and micas to again bronze out
like Maine's summer light.

And doing only this and that,
we talked of black-green pods,
the sand-studded weed and wood, and shell
the color of a boy's rose cheeks
in this Maine light, and the wide
relaxing light, the light itself,
more calm than lower light,
than palm and live oak light,
and talked of what tomorrow we'd find:
a glistening of seals, the thunder rock,

and nothing but such things as this,
this idle stuff that dances time,
all time turning, light to dark to light to dark,
time twirling in its repeating wheel,
that turns even the dumbest ticking of jagged gears
into a gloried and lambent joy.

* * *

Man in splendor's no easy concept now,
and Europe's green is made fertile with flesh.
At the wheat's root burns
what was once a child.
It is shame we sickle to mill
and shame we break to eat.
This is the loam of children,
the humus of their voices.
Such earth cannot credence the lie
of renewals and returns
and death the warm mother.
There is no return,
no warmth but the compost's,
no good come from our time.
The earth is not increased;
nothing is renewed;
everything is lessened.

Time's turned carrion-keeper in our time,
the clerk of cruelty

ledgering libraries of the unspeakable,
but you would not think it so,
would not doubt the splendid
were you here on this coast with me this morning
watching my son watching the cold tides
in light breathing out over the bay.

* * *

From my window and through the sway
of old ecru, I see them on the shore,
children who at such distance seem
slips and moving brights of color
carrying their pails and shells, busy
with sand's easy commerce.

Such scenes seem at such remove
from the branchings desire will take:
the minking up of the thighs, the sleek,
acrid heat of inflorescence and yearning;
blond boys' crownings out in the rerouting
of joys. But I'd wish innocence
on no one but children, would not hold
from my son the frenzy and driving
or desire's assumption of the heart,
biology turned mystery, the heavy paws
of need, and the incomprehensible lexicon
of lust; haze and indistinction, slips

rippling behind curtains, bafflement
at having been led till now by purpose,
led to a clear shore with sparkling sand.

* * *

All Maine's mornings are not alike,
not swept with the possibilities of red
above a harbor balancing miles of bright
fragmented foil on the undulating breath of the Atlantic.
In some there is a quickening in the light and air,
a brightness and cold flashing,
like the lifting of sails in the wind
and the wind's catching of white
and the rapid-riding out;
the full speed of men fluent in knots
looping the thick ropes like kite strings,
winding and whipping them into language
in the numbed, platinum light
of descended clouds and silent sun.

* * *

Last night spanning out in slow glide,
gulls dipped and called. The moon
spangled down, flared from the orange rouge
of old ladies smelling of talc, their lips
fragrant with glycerin and rose water,
to a pure blazing—intense as lead just cooled,

while lilac in fade and flame on the air recalled
the thin linen of ladies' handkerchiefs,
so thick with scent they tumbled
to the cool bottoms of black purses
big as Bibles, tumbled
with gloves and currency to wait,
to be drawn out, to infuse the air
like that lilac'd cool that came
coursing in with tides and gulls
and memories of my grandmother,
who would have given whole years
to have been here for a moment
just to have put her hand
into his golden, moon-marked curls.

* * *

There is another Maine.
It also curves the shore
in generous and prospering light.
But it is not the same;
this is the Maine of outlet stores
and flea markets, of miles of shacks of junk,
all clustering the same glittering shore.

Green brontosaurs rear up from miniature golf courses
and peer out at the highway; tipsy lobsters
bow-tied and in tails dance on the sides
of highway bars; and giant bears

atop concrete waterfalls look down
at the rows of campers rolling up
from America into Maine.

Into the ideal the tawdry always intrudes;
the hills of wild lupines give way;
the shorelines give way;
the delicate bays surrender their charm.

In the amusement park by the zoo
where I take my son, I watch
bumper cars collide and tattooed kids
fondle each other. His hand
is under her blouse; she rubs
her middle finger along his zipper.
They're both so unwashed
there's no thrill to watching.

My son pets the Vietnamese potbellied pigs.
For a quarter he gets a handful of feed.
Signs encourage children to feed the animals.
A deer too full to rise sits and lets him stroke
its fuzzing antlers. It does not like
the feel of a child's fingers on its tender horn,
jerks its head but does not rise.

Nothing here in this Maine rises
once having settled in. The lupines
are mowed and paved over; the chestnuts' flambeaux

extinguished in their fellings; the rhododendrons
graveled down. All that lifts into the air here
is the smell of grease and batter. Nothing
will rise again. This is the Maine
bent to Mammon, that peels and cracks
and is replastered and repainted
so brontosaurs and bears can forever stare down,
lobsters frolic, and new pigs and deer
be brought in when the others' arteries
squeeze shut, and no one notices, and no one
notices that anything has changed,
that anything has ever changed.

* * *

> *Þe tyme þat ic in lijf has lende*
> *in idel-nes ic haue it spende.*
> *—from* Cursor Mundi, *a Northumbrian poem, circa 1300*

Here where light and lilac,
air and bouldered shore meld
to mark the coast of Maine,
and beauty's lyric and blossoming,
the three of us in idle light
toy with time, dare tides to touch
our feet, and wander green streets
where architecture is precise as the air
and chestnuts in Amazonian abundance
outflower Provence; here where time's

at our wills' wishing in bright and idle light,
I wonder who with more talent for metaphor
than happiness first cast the grand equation,
first felt he'd spent or wasted joy's doing,
believed it convertible to coin or ash, saw time
as money, and thought days in lilac light
might be bettered in prayer or commerce.
Some Larkinesque medieval, I guess.
And I can hear him with his "What about
Mondays" and "What'll you do when
the vacation's over?" To set the present
against the future, to make time joy's spoiler
is like a taste for birch and leather, a vice
and misery there seems no casting out
of those for whom happiness is gall and boredom.

* * *

In primary light things are clarified;
knowledge is optic and immediate,
so obvious its utterance is commonplace:
as when I watched my son being born
and knew the truth of a hundred tritenesses;
or that day I lifted him and dislocated
his shoulder and felt fear and frenzy
with a knotting thick as fists; or when we sat
beneath a cool purity of light
and I watched him toss the largest stones
he could lift and call my attention

to each splash, and I remembered another beach,
another . . . oh, the obvious, the obvious:
when I remembered that love and light equate,
and that in this incandescence he kindles
I am defined, that in such definition,
such a showering of clear light,
I see billions of girls and boys
in his brilliant and burnished curls.

Self-portrait after Stanley Spencer

You have no idea how hard it is to live out
a great romance.
—Wallis Windsor

———————————

I.

It's not so difficult, really.
And I'd guess that plowing
or the laying of brick,
row on row, or the securing
of a steel axle might damage
more of some fine genealogical
delicacy or comfortable ease
than all love's labors compounded.

It's not so difficult, I think.
Attending enslaves only the selfish.
And joy is the product of stability's
clockwork. The monotonous grinding
of love's gears perpetually renews.
Ecstasy can be cultivated
like peas: Mendels of love
made free in the laws of attendance.

2.

In the abundance of her flesh and help,
she stretches the length of the canvas,
secures edges, sees to his centering,
and holds more than half his gaze.
He watches his toys float in space,
thinks himself haloed in the *et ceteras*
of his obsessions. But in her solid span
they are dwarfed down to nothing,
and the viewer is unaware even
of the brown paint-outs, the receding shadows.
Here is a man born to luck.
The ability to paint out the heart's slough
is his luck. She is his luck,
and her attendance is his keeping and his joy.

3.

Jacketed, earmuffed, and gloved,
I'd go into the garden
to drive my grandmother's pitchfork
into the frozen ground
between the hydrangeas. I'd pull up
thick chunks of earth
to taste the ice that had crystaled
inches down in the dark. And I'd dig

and play until I'd hear my grandmother's knuckles
against the steamed windowpanes
of her kitchen calling me in.

It's January again, and I am perhaps now
half-done with this accidental blessing.
A bead of sweat this moment drips down
from the kitchen window. The child
still turns the frozen earth. The grandmother
still calls him in. Everything
is gone; everything is whole;
everything is blessed.

for Carol

The Iowa Poetry Prize Winners

1987
Elton Glaser, *Tropical Depressions*
Michael Pettit, *Cardinal Points*

1988
Bill Knott, *Outremer*
Mary Ruefle, *The Adamant*

1989
Conrad Hilberry, *Sorting the Smoke*
Terese Svoboda, *Laughing Africa*

1993
Tom Andrews, *The Hemophiliac's Motorcycle*
Michael Heffernan, *Love's Answer*
John Wood, *In Primary Light*

The Edwin Ford Piper Poetry Award Winners

1990
Philip Dacey, *Night Shift at the Crucifix Factory*
Lynda Hull, *Star Ledger*

1991
Greg Pape, *Sunflower Facing the Sun*
Walter Pavlich, *Running near the End of the World*

1992
Lola Haskins, *Hunger*
Katherine Soniat, *A Shared Life*